soulsister wellness

ruth dive

laura evans

authors
AND CO.

ISBN13 Paperback: 978-1-915771-08-7

contents

introduction

We realised in the planning of SoulSister Wellness back in early 2021 that teenage girls really needed more support in their understanding of how they can take control of their own emotional and physical health outcomes.

Fast forward to the end of 2021 and we decided to launch a very special project – *Look at Me Now!* – inviting ten local teenage girls to work with us for a year. There was a commitment from us to inspire confidence and resilience, sharing knowledge about the power of making healthy choices and offering mentoring with local businesswomen to provide the girls with aspirations for their futures.

In April 2022 we went on to launch a workshop version of this programme for schools and have since gone on to work with almost five hundred teenage girls.

Our overriding aim has always been to try to improve the emotional and physical health outcomes of young people, but what we quickly realised was that the issues that these girls faced and so openly shared with us were so powerful if only they could have the confidence to share them with each other.

This collection of words and advice has come from our ten very special girls who have shown so much courage in sharing their own stories to help others.

Our message is that every single person has a story and that those stories can bind us together to help us through our own. When we give others the chance to open up, we see that we can all be connected to help each other.

We are so very proud and thank you for supporting their work.

Ruth & Laura x

about the authors

Soul Sister Wellness CIC is an organisation founded by Ruth Dive and Laura Evans.

Based in North Wales, they work with young people to educate and empower them with ways to support their own health and wellbeing outcomes in life.

As well as offering workshops, programmes and 1-2-1 sessions in the community and online, they also deliver talks and workshops in both primary and high schools.

Ruth's background is coaching, Neuro Linguistic Programming, Heart Healing and hypnotherapy, with Laura providing nutrition, wellness and health coaching.

Outside of work Ruth will probably be found out walking with her beautiful family and 2 dogs. A lover of sunsets, adventures and pretty views. Happy to finish sentences with a kiss instead of a full stop.... happy to be different.

Laura is passionate about creating healthy family meals at home and spending as much time outdoors with her gorgeous family and dogs.

A lover of sunrise, she'll be found in early morning fitness bootcamps and hiking up a mountain as often as she can.

facebook.com/TheSoulSisterWellness
instagram.com/the.ssw

healthy friendships

. . .

Elise

DEAR FRIEND,

My name is Elise and I'm currently a Year Eight student. If you're about to join secondary school, your head is most likely spinning with lots of scary and exciting thoughts right now. I'm here to say that you're not alone at all.

You are most likely worrying about difficulties with your friends or friendship group, wondering if you will fit in, will people like you in the new school, etc. which are all perfectly normal feelings. Most people suffer with this in high school and it's never different in any other high school and that's why I'm here to help you through that or to get you prepared for it.

It is not always easy in high school. In fact, it can be really hard sometimes, but you can never forget that you have got your family and friends that will always be by your side through all of it. It's not only you that's feeling scared, worried, emotional and nervous; there are so many girls and boys that are feeling the same.

I was a very anxious, worried and emotional Year Six girl who was about to start high school. I started in September 2020 – the Covid year, so I didn't get to finish primary school properly and had no transition days before I started high school. This was very scary for me, as I had not seen my primary school friends for months. I had all sorts of thoughts and emotions swirling around in my head, wondering if those friends were still my friends, and whether they still liked me. What if they left me for new friends and I was on my own? I was a bit of an emotional wreck if I am being completely honest. I was so afraid and I was experiencing the worst feelings I had ever felt in my childhood.

If you are experiencing the same feelings as me, I completely understand as I have felt them. This is totally normal. But I'm telling you that as soon as you get to your school you will probably be fine. Your move to high school may be problem free. For others there may be a few hurdles along the way, but with the right support from family and friends, there is a way out of them, and you will get through this. You will meet lots of new friends along the way, some that remain your friends and some that don't. As time goes by, you will learn who your people are. They will be the ones that are most likely to have the same interests and hobbies as you. Friends who have your back, friends who support you and build you up. I find meeting new people is always very interesting.

Now I'm going to tell you about my story in high school and what I experienced with friends.

When I was in Year Seven, I made lots of new friends, a whole group of them. Everything was going great until the day I was turned against by some of the girls within the group. I was being ganged up on and I had no idea why.

It all started when I was away on holiday with my family. I noticed that my friends were not texting me or replying to my messages. I was just being ignored! I had spent the day with my friends the day before I went away and we had a lovely time. At first, I just thought maybe it was because I was away on holiday with my family and they didn't want to disturb me.

It was time to go back to school after the holidays and it was then that I realised that it wasn't all in my head and that friends were actually ignoring me. My two best friends were becoming closer with each other and were leaving me out. They just didn't talk back to me and didn't include me at break time.

A group chat was made which I was added to, but it was just set up for them to have a go at me. They would say that I was talking badly about them to other people. A picture of me was posted on the group chat and nasty comments were made about me. They would recruit other friends within the group to dislike me. Other friends within the group would message me trying to trick me into saying things about these girls.

Luckily, I was wise to this so didn't give them what they wanted. I would be shoulder barged in the corridors at school. They would move their chairs away from me in the classroom and on one occasion, I had food thrown at me at dinner time. This went on for weeks.

I was really confused by all of this. I didn't understand how people can be so cruel. Before going to school, I would feel so sick that I couldn't eat. I would start sweating at the very thought of having to face them. I became very quiet and a lot less talkative and felt quite withdrawn. I have never experienced this before, so these feelings were very new to me. I was very emotional and felt all alone. I took a step back from social media, as this would be used to target me. A few weeks later, everything settled down and they wanted to be my friend again. I went along with it: anything for a quiet life, I thought.

I started Year Eight and things had settled within the friendship group. Everything was going great again until after Christmas when there was more drama within the friendship group. Some of the boys I was friends with were making horrible comments about how I look, saying that I have an ugly figure and that I was just ugly in general. I had a feeling that these comments were driven by a couple of the girls I had had problems with before, as they were with the boys when they made these comments and they didn't defend me. I gradually started to notice that they were being different with me.

I was part of a group chat in which these girls started to be horrible to me again. They were using the same old reason, saying that I was talking badly about them. I left the group, as I couldn't be bothered to go through this again. One of the girls then messaged me the following day to ask if we could be friends again. I was a bit reluctant but said ok.

A few days after this, I was added to another group in which they targeted me again. Lots of things were posted on social media about me, saying things such as, "When is she going to get that nobody likes her," and that they were going to smash my face in. I felt as though my life was falling apart around me, I felt totally broken and all alone.

My worst fears about starting high school all came true. Things became more challenging in all aspects of my life. Within my family life, I was just very angry with everyone and when my parents tried to talk to me, I would just shut them out. I would slam doors, I would scream at them and say some awful things, such as "Go away", "Leave me alone" and, "Your opinion doesn't matter. I don't care what you think." I would just stay in my room and cry. I hated myself for behaving like this, but I had no control over how I was feeling.

I was at my worst point when I decided to self-harm. It made me have something else to focus on rather than think about everything that was happening around me. I didn't like myself very much, so didn't care about scarring myself. I didn't care about what people thought either. I started to question if there was something wrong with me, because I was always the target. I even started to wear false eyelashes and tan because of the "ugly" comments. People thought I did it because I was insecure, but it made me feel like I fitted in. I wanted to make myself look like the other girls to be accepted.

School work became extremely challenging. I couldn't concentrate and found work really difficult. I had no interest in school whatsoever as it just reminded me of bad things. I did try to defend myself on many occasions, whether it be to their faces or via text but they wouldn't believe me. I was diagnosed as having dyslexia in Year Seven, so whenever I confronted these people, I would always end up feeling embarrassed as they would use better words than me or would make fun if I spelled a word wrong.

I became a really unhappy person, less motivated and tried to get out of going to school by faking illnesses. I really struggled to trust anyone, for fear of just getting hurt all over again. All of this made a huge dent in my confidence in the way I performed at school, the way I acted and the way I looked.

Everything started to calm down after a couple of months of going through hell. The moment of change for me was when I decided to talk to my family about it rather than shutting them out. Offloading all of my problems made me feel so much better. My family are my safe space and knowing that I had their support got me through this.

I also became close to one of my friends who I had grown apart from because of the drama at school. She had experienced something similar at school and was really supportive towards me. Knowing that I had a friend who understood really made a difference and helped me to get through this. It made me realise that there are nice people out there. It made me happy again.

I also knew that the people that were being unkind to me would also want to be my friend again when they could see that I was getting on with my life and being happy. The one thing I have learned from this is that people who are horrible to you are only that way because they don't like themselves or their life and just want to make other people miserable. The nasty comments made about how you look are only made by people who don't like themselves. It is their way of venting their frustrations. Once I understood this, it made me feel better about myself and made me realise that I wasn't the problem.

At the moment I feel happy with my new friends. I still talk to the girls that were bullying me. I'm just not close with them any more as they have lost my trust. I've learnt that every time I get triggered by these people, it just makes me much stronger.

My feelings are so much happier now. I thought I could overcome or find a way out of bullying by self-harming but that was the worst decision I ever made. The best way to overcome situations like this are by saying to yourself, "They are just jealous and aren't happy in their life." People that do this are just pathetic and want to make your life miserable because they're not happy.

I am currently part of a project group with other teenage girls. The aim is to build resilience, self-love, confidence and self-esteem and have healthy habits. This is really helping me to deal with these situations. The group focuses on the importance of liking you for who you are, to be yourself and to not be influenced by anyone. I am now starting to realise all of these things, and although I am not 100% there, I would say that I am now in a much better place than when I first joined the group. The girls that run the group are so lovely and accept us all for who we are. I feel very lucky to have had this opportunity; it really has made a difference.

Right now, you may be feeling a bit overwhelmed by my story and find it a bit daunting. You may be feeling a bit scared and worried, thinking that this may happen to you. Remember that these experiences are not going to last. It is how you deal with them that's important.

It will knock your confidence and you will experience low self-esteem. It will also have an impact on your emotional wellbeing, as it did with me. The best way to overcome these challenging times is by opening up to people you trust. Talk to people who see you as being important in their life, people who will not judge.

You need to be kind to yourself, be optimistic and find a good strong friendship group. It is important to work on your own resilience as life is full of obstacles.

I am now starting to recognise what a healthy friendship is and that is a friend who genuinely wants to be your friend. Find friends who are not jealous of you and respect you. Life is just so much more fun once you have this.

I still talk to the girls who gave me a hard time, but I now know my self-worth. I have learned to respond differently by ignoring anything negative.

Be positive in your own ability, goals and strengths. You will go through a process of change in your attitude and feelings. There is no quick recovery. However, by getting the right support, in time, I promise you will get there.

life is tough, but so are you

. . .

Evie

DEAR FRIEND,

Being a teenager is tough, right? They never really prepare you for the challenging years to come. There is no certain guidebook that you are supposed to follow. We are all just 'winging' it every single day. We all have our own ways of overcoming things, and it is sometimes good as we can learn from our experiences.

The teenage years are especially hard as you transition into high school. You start to find true friends and maybe some not so loyal friends. It can be a very tough and exhausting time being a teenager and we all have our own ways of getting through it. None of us are perfect, but that is what makes us all so unique in our special way.

Anxiety can be an added pressure to the already nerve-racking thought of high school. High school is a worrying thought on its own, but the added pressure of having anxiety could possibly make it even worse. It is a scary thing, starting high school for the first time, especially like making friends and being comfortable with the new environment that you are in. Me especially, I find change a difficult thing due to my anxiety and transitioning to high school can be a very nervous period of time if you don't like change. Making friends is also a very scary time for people with anxiety whilst starting high school, but trust me, you will make friends and you will find people who you are comfortable with.

I suffer from anxiety, which is especially hard in the school environment as that is what most of my anxiety is based on. It is also hard when experiencing anxiety when you don't know who your true friends are, as you really need people to be there and reassure you that everything will be okay. I was very nervous when I was starting high school as I was not sure if I would be able to make friends and my anxiety also added to the paranoia and the stress of making friends.

But I was just myself and I did not let my anxiety prevent me from talking to new people and I made a lot of new friends by getting out of my comfort zone and talking to new people. I promise you that you are not the only one who feels like this and there are plenty of other people scared about going into high school.

If you go up to people and start talking to them, they could potentially be very happy and relieved that you have talked to them. Other people may also be too scared to talk to new people and if you never speak to each other, then you could miss out on making a new friend. You will find lots of new friends who you will feel comfortable with and who will be there for you when you need them.

I am one of those people who find it quite hard to be able to trust people. I think that is another part of my anxiety where I start to overthink things so much to the point where it is too much. It is also just hard when people don't realise how much their words can mean and affect an over-thinker as they will constantly be thinking about what you have said to them and the true meaning behind it.

I feel like sometimes I can be quite sensitive. Also, sometimes I think I take what people say to me to heart. This can sometimes be sort of a bad thing, as I start to overthink about it and wonder, "What if they don't like me? Have I done something wrong?" But I also feel like when you are overthinking, people can be a bit inconsiderate whilst you are overthinking everything and just don't think about others at times.

In high school, I think that is when I started to develop anxiety. It wasn't just an overnight thing. I just started to panic and freak out about things. This was all new to me as believe it or not, I was quite confident when I was younger. I think that in school especially, it can be a very testing environment to feel like you fit in. I think that anyone with anxiety or something like this will be able to agree, but it is so frustrating when people use the term, "------- is giving me anxiety." This can be very frustrating for someone who suffers from anxiety as a certain thing does not give you anxiety; you have to already have anxiety to be able to have it in a certain situation. Part of my anxiety means that I can suffer from panic attacks and that sometimes can happen in school when there is a test or even when I just get really stressed.

Due to my anxiety, I can get very stressed and worried in the school environment, and it can feel like I am alone at times. The pressure of tests for someone who does not suffer from anxiety can be stressful enough. However, for someone who does suffer from anxiety it can be a lot of stress that overcomes you all in one period of time. Trying to juggle all of the pressures of school and the added weight of anxiety can be very overwhelming at times. But, whatever happens, I always overcome it, so I know for sure that you will definitely be able to overcome anything.

When I was thirteen years old, my mum got married to her now husband. I feel like this was a very confusing time for me as there is always a stigma around 'step' relatives. I personally do not say 'stepdad', but I just choose to call my mum's husband by his name and refer to him as 'my mum's husband'. I feel like this is perfectly fine and that anyone who is going through the same thing that I have been through just needs to know that everything will be okay, and this confusion stage will not go on forever. You will still find time to spend with your biological parent and I still see my dad and I love my dad to bits.

The added pressures of having to control the balance between home life and school life can also be a difficult time. School can be a very testing and worrying time, but then also you have the events that happen at home that add to the stresses of school. Anxiety can happen in all aspects of your life. It is not just in the school environment; it can occur everywhere in life. But everything happens for a reason and my friends in school were there for me. It is okay if your friends cannot always relate to you situation. It is just important that they are there for you whenever you need them.

Around October of 2021, I decided that what would benefit me, was to maybe try out counselling sessions. I think that those sessions have helped me massively, I feel more confident and they have taught me key coping techniques when I do feel anxious and worried.

Another stigma that I absolutely hate is the stigma around counselling and therapy. More and more people are putting their mental health as a priority, which is the right thing. I feel like mental health should be a more openly spoken topic, as especially over the past few years, mental health is more important than ever. Most people nowadays suffer from poor mental health, and I think that we need to normalise the term "mental health" and reassure people that it is perfectly normal and fine to have difficulties.

Although I still suffer from anxiety, I feel that I have found some coping mechanisms and I do not get so stressed over school anymore. I have learned the fact that it is okay not to have everything under control and to just 'go with' things that are happening. I have learned not to let things that I cannot change stress me out, and that if there is nothing I can do to change it, then I should not be worrying about it.

This progress has not just happened overnight; it has taken me a long time to come to terms with this.

When you are feeling a sense of panic that comes rushing over, it is always important to remember to remain calm. That is the best thing to be able to do in a stressful situation. Some coping mechanisms I like to use are to embrace your surroundings and really focus on what is around you and it will take your mind off your panicking and stress. This will help you to really calm yourself and you can even turn it into a game, such as 'try and see how many purple objects you can spot'. This then tricks your mind and you are slowly able to calm yourself.

Another key coping mechanism I find really helpful is to focus on my breathing. When I begin to panic, my breathing begins to increase at a really fast rate and makes me panic even more. I find that 'box breathing' really helps me calm down in stressful situations. This is where you breathe in for four counts, hold it for four counts, breathe out for four counts, and then hold for four counts. This really helps me to slow my breathing and I become more relaxed and panic less to be able to overcome the difficult situation. If you are ever in a stressful situation, maybe you could try one of these techniques and see if it helps you to calm down.

Ten tips for teenagers:

1. Never dwell on your 'imperfections'; those are the things that make you 'perfect'.
2. You have great ambitions and aspirations in life, so never EVER let anyone tell you otherwise.
3. Always trust your instinct. If you think that someone is not a nice friend, then they are probably not. Try to find people that deserve your friendship and kindness.
4. Everything will get better, trust me. Yes, things will be tough and you might really struggle. But everything works out in the end, and if it hasn't, then it is not the end.
5. You will eventually find friends who will appreciate you as much as you appreciate them. Sometimes it can feel like you have no one, but trust me, it just takes time.
6. The challenges you face now will prepare you for later in life.
7. Write your feelings down. I find it difficult to talk and communicate sometimes due to my anxiety, and so I find it very beneficial to write down how I am feeling as a way to get it off my chest.

8. Everything will be okay (I think I sometimes need to be reminded about that) but just remember that it will all be okay and although it might seem like the end of the world at the time, you have so much waiting for you in life.
9. Be yourself. If people don't like the real you, then it is their loss that they don't get to know you.
10. Remember that everything happens for a reason and trust the process of life. Good things are coming your way.

I feel that I am a more confident person now and I am more confident within myself. I do still get a bit sad at times and that is normal to feel those emotions. However, I am not sad for long as I manage to pick myself up and find the main cause of why I am sad. By doing this I can make sure that I don't feel down for too long. I feel that I am more relaxed as well and you too can feel like this. I know sometimes it can feel like it is the end of the world. But I guarantee that your feelings will soon subside and you too will become more confident and come out as a happier and stronger person.

I know at the moment that you may feel like you will never be able to feel confident and content with yourself again. But I guarantee that you will come out of this stage and be stronger and will be happy with yourself. These feelings that you are feeling at the moment will not last forever. You will soon be happy and will find people who you are comfortable with. I know that you will go on to achieve your dreams and this stage is a part of you that will make you a stronger and better person in the end.

I wish you all the best in the future and I know you will achieve great things.

Evie

just believe in yourself

. . .

Jasmine

DEAR FRIEND,

I understand what you might be going through right now. There are some emotions you may be experiencing or perhaps some that you've never even felt before. Anger, sadness, that gut feeling in your stomach or when your throat gets tight and feels like it's going to close. It's okay to feel like that. Nobody's perfect, we all have our good and bad days, even adults.

Social media is tough. Do you find yourself constantly feeling that what you're seeing is true and that the person that you're looking at has a perfect life? Or maybe you feel that you have to fit a certain standard, to not be different and to be the same as everybody else? Maybe you feel the pressure of needing to look like these models and wanting their features instead of accepting yourself and being an individual. This is the mindset of young girls nowadays and it lowers their confidence and self-esteem by the day.

Social media. It is one of the most popular things used on our mobiles in our lives today and leaves a massive impact on people, mainly teenagers. The most common things that social media can do is make us compare ourselves and can make us feel jealous of another person and their appearance.

Instagram is probably one of the biggest examples of this. I open up the app, I scroll, I can see pictures of these girls, models, they're beautiful. They look perfect. Then I zoom in and study the picture harder and then the questions come... Why can't my teeth look like that? Why can't my face look like that? Why doesn't my body look like that? Why can't my body shape be like that? And you just continuously ask yourself these questions over and over again. Why can't I look like 'them'? Why can't I be 'them'? Why don't I look like 'them'? 'Them' becomes a person who is perfect in my vision.

This is where the behind the scenes come in. 'Them' is edited and fake. Maybe their teeth aren't actually that white – they've just edited it because they're scared of judgment. Maybe their body doesn't look like that – they've just edited it to look like the other 'thems'. Maybe their face doesn't actually look like that –they've just added a filter in case they get 'judged'. Everyone has their own unique and individual insecurities, even me and possibly, even you.

For me, it all began a couple of years ago. I didn't really know what was happening at first. I was just doing what a normal teenage girl does, scrolling on Instagram and liking pictures of my friends. 'Wow, she's so pretty,' I would think, or, 'I want to look like her.' Sometimes I thought, 'I look so ugly compared to her.'

At first, I felt guilty of having these thoughts, but I ignored them. After a while I didn't feel bad or guilty for telling myself these things any more. 'Wow she's so pretty,' 'I want to look like her,' 'I look so ugly compared to her,'... these words became more frequent in my head every single day, even when I wasn't looking at the pictures. It was all I could think about. In school, at home, when I was with my friends, when I was at dance class. The thoughts started to become louder in my head as if they were shouting at me; the thoughts kept coming and coming.

'I would die to look like her,' I began thinking. 'My body looks big compared to her,' or even, 'I hate how I look.' They just kept getting worse and worse; it was never ending. It got to the point where I felt really anxious a lot. I was scared to open up the app in case I got upset by these thoughts and feelings. I felt anxious walking in public and in the corridors at school. I felt like everyone was watching me and secretly judging me for how I look. Judging how I don't look like 'them'. It was just a never-ending cycle that I was trapped in and couldn't escape. A cycle of thoughts and emotions. Repeating itself. All it did was get worse.

Things became a lot more challenging. I started to feel really angry with myself because I had no control over changing my appearance. I couldn't look at myself in the mirror without crying and being disgusted with the way I look. I didn't want to go out, I didn't want to go to school. I checked all the comments on my posts. 'You're so gorgeous!' or 'How are you so pretty?' they would say. Surely, they weren't about me. They were probably just saying that to make me feel good or because they wanted to be polite. I never accepted a compliment because I knew it was fake because I don't look like 'them'.

This is where it got bad. That's all I was doing, comparing myself. I hated everything about myself. It's all I cared about. It wrecked me mentally. I just felt so useless and ugly. I tried everything but even makeup didn't cover it this time. I felt lost and hurt inside. Nobody understood me. 'Why are you always upset over social media just because you're insecure and you compare yourself to the other girls?' But it wasn't that easy.

The harder part was that it got so addictive to look at pictures of these girls but being addicted to social media was horrible. I was upset all the time, constantly crying and getting angry. It just made me feel even worse by the second because the more I thought about it, the bigger the thoughts got. It got really hard to stop looking at these pictures because I just thought how good I would feel in myself if I looked like all these people on social media, how confident and how high my self-esteem would be. Just imagining the feeling of looking that way hurt a lot.

Over time I noticed a lack in my confidence and the way I treated myself and a massive decrease in my mood. It affected me quite a lot. It hasn’t always been easy but after long time of comparison I came to realise that sitting in my room crying constantly about the way I look and that I don’t look like everyone else wasn’t helping and let's be real, it was just making the situation a whole lot worse. I finally decided to speak to someone who I trust, my mum. For you it could be a parent, a friend, a teacher or just any adult or person you trust. I told my mum how social media made me feel and how pressured I've felt by it. When we sat and talked about it, I recognized that nobody is perfect – everybody is unique.

All of this comes down to mindset, but you have to work towards it. You couldn’t just wake up one day and decide, “I'm not going to compare myself ever again.” You may think that, but your guard is going to fall and you're going to start and begin the cycle again. To start to work towards your mindset change and to make it positive, whenever you do see someone that you ‘want to look like’ you’ve got to think ‘hold on: most of it is edited and fake’ and ‘nobody's perfect so why should I be like them when I'm happy with myself?' There may be a couple of things that I don't like about myself, but it doesn't mean I have to put everyone down and make myself feel bad and guilty just because of my insecurities. We can work past them; you can learn to love them instead of looking to change or compare.

Next time you go on a social media platform, for example Instagram, instead of comparing again or being jealous, support the person instead. Even if it's something little it could make a person's day. Instead of thinking, 'I want to look like them and be like them,' you say to them, 'I like that outfit on you,' or 'You look really nice.' This is a lot more positive than putting yourself down.

Once I started doing this it felt weird at first and was quite hard, but over time, as I kept doing it more often, it felt like I was a whole new person. I find that I'm a lot happier without all those tears and jealousy and I also find I'm a lot more confident in myself. When I'm out I do still have the odd wobble, for example, if I don't like what I'm wearing today, the thought of people staring at me means they are 'judging' me, but in reality, they're not, they're just minding their own business and getting on with their own day.

Right now, I am a lot happier with myself and how far I've come considering that I was really bad with the impacts of social media and wanting to be like/look like other people. It's now less stressful and one less thing to worry about. To people who are experiencing similar things to me, I highly recommend having a go at changing your mindset and the way you think about things. Like I've said it was hard to start with and I wanted to give up the positivity, but you've just got to put the effort into it and work towards it in order to get to the stage where I'm at now. So instead of thinking you want to be someone else, support that someone else and be happy for them but also support yourself. Instead of turning away from the mirror, look in it and say something positive to yourself even though you might not believe yourself at first. Over time your mind will gradually change to make you believe it; therefore, it will leave a positive impact on you and hopefully will make you feel a lot happier.

Always remember to check on the ones close to you. You never know what they might be going through. It's so easy to hide behind a mask. Perhaps they act all happy and smiley on the outside but deep down they just want to say, 'I'm not okay.' We need to start being there for each other and letting others know that no matter what, you will always have their back.

Right now, you may be feeling confused, sad and angry with yourself. Remember that you're not alone and these feelings will pass. To help bring the positive mindset into place, try turning this around by writing a list of all your positive qualities. Your kindness and uniqueness are what make you beautiful. The most important words are those you say to yourself – be kind.

Each morning when you wake up, try and say three positive affirmations about yourself and believe in them, for example: *I am loved, I am capable,* and *I can cope* or even *I believe in myself.* Just by doing this every day, it will make you start to feel more confident in yourself. You will get through this, if you just believe in yourself.

trauma doesn't have to mean the end

. . .

Lexie

DEAR FRIEND,

If you are being bullied, I bet you must be feeling a mixture of emotions right now. You'll be finding it difficult to sleep at night, but when you do wake up to the alarm clock you are nowhere near ready to wake up because it feels like you've only had five minutes of sleep. The nights really are so long, aren't they? This is the time when everything goes round and round in your head and you play out the different situations over and over again.

Morning finally arrives, the day begins again, and you seem to be in this vicious cycle of emotions. One minute you're feeling ok, and the next your stomach is in knots and you feel angry. You don't know if this due to the lack of sleep or due to what you're going through and the situation. Either way, it causes so much stress and makes you feel worthless and miserable. I mean, you're depressed one minute and happy the next and then trying to find the energy to do daily tasks. Even taking a shower takes so much effort. You're finding it hard to concentrate because your head is so full of what's going on – you struggle to take anything else in. Sometimes it feels like your head is about to explode and you feel like shutting the whole world out.

The pain that you are feeling in your head and your heart feels never ending. It feels like you're in a vicious circle that's going on for what seems like decades. I completely understand how you're feeling. Believe me when I say you are not alone. I have been there too. I used to wake up and pray to God to guide me out of this dark place.

However, now I wake up and thank God that he wrapped his arms around me and I'm still here. I used to tell myself I was worthless and thought I would be better off dead. For the first time in my life, I was experiencing the most awful anxiety. I used to bite the inside of my cheek, leaving me with horrendous ulcers. I didn't know until lately that this is a form of self-harm. However, at the time I didn't realize I was doing it until it was extremely sore, but uncomfortable situations such as meeting new people or thinking back to what had happened made me do it all the more. At my lowest point I hit rock bottom, but thankfully I'm in a much better place now.

I'd like to take you back to when it all began in April 2021. I was just thirteen years old. You might be wondering what a thirteen-year-old could possibly have to tell you. However, I have experienced things that a lot of adults may not have even experienced. I really didn't have the best time at school. Some say school gives you the best years of your life. However, my own experiences tell me differently!

I went to an all-girls school. As you can imagine, all girls in a school together can cause its own set of problems. The bullying at school started gradually. At first, I thought I was just being sensitive, yet it was the same group of girls that continuously went out of their way to make sure I didn't fit in or belong with anyone. It was a combination of loads of little things that gradually built up to the point where it became unbearable.

It started with something as simple as saying, "You can't sit with us," but that was not good enough for them – they wanted to hurt me even more. The girl I was sitting with was encouraged to join them, which then left me on my own. I had a toilet pass that went missing from my bag and then I had books also go missing from my locker. The group of girls would start sniggering and laughing when I had to explain to the teacher that I didn't have my books. Teachers started questioning me, asking why I kept misplacing my things.

From all the stress I started getting such bad migraines that my mum took me to the opticians and then to the doctors. It was stress that was causing these headaches. My mum could tell I was really struggling and made the decision to home school me.

You'd think that being home schooled would make all the problems disappear, but this was not the case and worse by far was yet to come.

I had the best summer in 2021. I met up with a new friend and we truly had the best time and made so many memories.

I had very stupidly made the mistake of sending a nude picture of my boobs to a boy that I really liked and who kept asking me for a photo. I had sent the picture to him the previous year, during the summer of 2020. I regretted it as soon as I sent it. This picture came back to haunt me in November 2021, when the boy sent it to that group of girls who had bullied me in school. These girls used social media to send me vile, nasty messages. I won't write what they said in the messages as I wouldn't want to give them any form of credit but as you can imagine they were extremely nasty, and my mum had to get the police involved.

I turned to my new friend and I was shocked by her response. She said she had absolutely no sympathy for me and couldn't have cared less. At the time I wasn't looking for her sympathy; I was just looking for her support. We argued a bit and then we put things aside and were friends again. I was so happy. I had a great Christmas of 2021 with my friend. We exchanged gifts and planned to meet up again on New Year's Eve. Everything was quiet with the group of girls until January fifth, 2022.

This was when my life got turned upside down. Earlier I said I hit rock bottom: here is why. On New Year's Eve 2021, my friend and I met up with this group of boys. Two of them were brothers, and we went to an organized house party. The party wasn't great so we all decided to leave. It was freezing cold and getting dark. Most shops of the were shutting. I decided to phone my mum and ask if we were all allowed back to the house.

Mum agreed to them coming back to the house for a little while so with that we all walked back to my house. My mum cooked pizza for us and went upstairs to lie down. One of the boys and I went upstairs to my room and had sex. During it, the boy's brother and his friend burst into my room with his phone in his hand. Unbeknown to me at the time, the phone was recording.

On the night of January fifth, 2022, I got added into an Instagram group chat by one of the boys from New Year's Eve. The group was made up of those boys, but also two of the girls that had bullied me at school. One of the boys sent the video of me having sex into the group chat. I honestly felt sick, and I didn't know what to do. The vicious, nasty comments they were making were just horrendous. I really can't understand how people can be that cruel and mean to one another.

I was scared. Scared of what my mum would say, scared of what people would think and even more scared of this video being shared.

I didn't know where to begin. I didn't even know how to start the conversation with my mum as I felt embarrassed and ashamed. At the time I could only see one way out and that was to end my life.

I took an overdose of a large quantity of paracetamol and WhatsApp messaged my mum saying, *I love you, Mum.* This message was enough for mum to know something wasn't right. She got out of bed and went downstairs to find me slumped on the sofa, shaking, with empty boxes of paracetamol by my side, drifting in and out of consciousness. I don't remember much more, other than waking up in the hospital and knowing that mum now knew about the video. The police were now involved. The crisis nurse that saw me was lovely and gave me so much reassurance.

By this point I felt as if a massive weight had been lifted off my shoulders as I didn't have to explain to mum what had happened. She'd seen the video and messages. Mum was extremely supportive and I couldn't ask for a better mum. She didn't judge me; my biggest fear was of being judged. I now had to tell the rest of my family… One of the biggest things was feeling like I had disappointed everyone. Thankfully I am surrounded by a loving and supportive family who all pull together when times are tough.

The next challenge I had to overcome was speaking to the police. I was very anxious that I would be judged by them. Two lady detectives came to my house to interview me to get a better understanding of what was going on. This was part of my turning point. They massively reassured me that none of this was my fault. I had to give a detailed explanation of what had happened on that night. They didn't make me feel embarrassed or ashamed. They made me see it was okay to speak up. I will always be grateful for the support and reassurance they gave me.

My best friend had heard the news of my suicide attempt by that time. She contacted me and we arranged to meet. Everybody that I knew who was aware of the video had been non-judgmental and supportive so I was kind of expecting the same thing from my friend. However, this was not the case. I started to tell her about the video and she burst out laughing, saying she knew all about the video and also knew they were videoing me on that night but chose not to do anything as she thought it was highly funny and would teach me a lesson. Knowing she could have stopped this made me feel sick to my stomach. Friends aren't supposed to be there to teach us lessons; friends are supposed to look out for each other. After her words to me, there was no way I could even begin to fix our friendship. I knew that it was the end for us and it was best for us to go our separate ways.

People were now sending me the video with crying-laughing emojis and asking if it was me. My biggest fear was happening. The video was now being shared. I was devastated. Not only had I lost my best friend, I felt as if I had lost myself too.

I found that going out on evening walks with my mum was the best way for me to talk freely about how I was feeling and what was going on inside my mind. I also found it helpful to talk to my social worker, who I saw once a fortnight for four months. My poor mum… I had her out walking all hours of the day and night, but this was when my lightbulb moments happened. I realized that everyone makes mistakes and it doesn't have to be the end of the world.

I started having counselling in April 2022. I really could have done with counselling back in January when it all happened, but the wait times are so long. I would encourage anyone going through anything to talk to their parents or an adult and don't go through it alone, because you don't have to. One bit of advice I have for you is don't expect everything to get better overnight. It's normal to have low days and days when you feel mentally drained and do not have the energy to do anything, but you need to push through those bad days, get up, shower, get dressed, and do the things that make you happy. The more time you spend sitting around, the worse you end up feeling. It's like being sucked into a dark hole. Although it may not feel like it at first, the more you're doing and keeping your mind busy, the better you will start to feel in yourself.

I'm not going to lie: those days aren't easy especially in the beginning when you're going through something traumatic and you want to shut the whole world out. Don't get me wrong, I still have days like that, but thankfully they are becoming fewer and fewer. The good days are starting to outweigh the bad days and I'm starting to feel like I'm finding myself again. I'm starting to laugh a lot more and trying not to take life too seriously.

I often enjoy having lunch in the garden and watching the clouds go by and looking to see what different shapes and images I can make out of them; I also love to watch the sunset and occasionally the sunrise.

Prior to my trauma taking place I'd started up my own little business, personalizing water bottles, hoodies, t-shirts etc. I called it TAGS.88888 (Tatey's Awesome Gift Shop). My confidence was at rock bottom, and I felt like what I was doing was no longer good enough, so I stepped back from it and took time out for a few months. I've slowly started to build it up again. I still have to overcome barriers and tell myself I am just as good as anyone else – and you are too!

I have found I do struggle to make friends and still suffer with anxiety. At one point I used to bite the inside of my cheek and would end up with big holes inside my mouth. After talking to my counsellor, I have only just realized that this is a form of self-harm. We talked about ways to cope with anxiety instead of biting my cheek and one that really worked for me was to put a hairband on my wrist and ping it against my wrist so it gives that bit of pain but isn't going to cause any permanent scars or any issues in the long term.

By this point I can imagine you must be feeling a mixture of emotions and that's perfectly normal. I have taken you through part of my journey which involved friendship, betrayal, nudity, having a pornographic video shared, bullying and attempted suicide. Life hasn't always been easy but it does get better.

You have to believe in yourself, and always share with someone how you're feeling because talking will somehow make you feel better. It might not feel like it at the time but talking is all part of helping you heal.

There are so many different things to experience in life and to look forward to and enjoy. Don't let anything or anyone hold you back and stop you from following your dreams. Sometimes horrible things happen in life, but you don't need to let them define you. You are still amazing, no matter what.

I'm more than grateful to be alive and writing this today. I hope by reading this it shows you that you're not alone and that it gives you the courage and strength to speak up. Trauma doesn't have to mean the end!

Never give up…

Lexie-Rose

you'll strengthen to walk the storm, not to fight it

. . .

Megan

DEAR FRIEND,

If you're experiencing trauma after an accident or the loss of a beloved friend (human or animal), then I want you to know that you are not on your own. You may be feeling anger, sadness or hatred or even all three at this moment in time, but what doesn't kill you makes you stronger. Do you ever feel as though you don't belong, or that you cannot cope anymore with losing someone you really love just because of the selfish acts of other people and their idiotic actions? Trust me, I really, really do know and understand what you are going through.

Sometimes you may feel as though there is no point in getting up in the mornings because someone you love or someone very dear to you won't be there to greet you, but then you remember all of the good times and the memories that you had together, or that all of the other animals need to be fed, watered and exercised (if the friend you've lost is an animal), and that is what powers your day. If you have any animals, remember that they could be missing the animal or person that you have lost as well, and by comforting them, they will comfort you!

You are not the only one to have felt this way. I am still going through all of the feelings and emotions that I mentioned above as I write this chapter for you. Up until two weeks ago – the end of May 2022 – I thought that my life was changing for the better but then due to a series of traumatic events, my life hopped back onto life's crazy roller coaster and my feelings and emotions turned for the worse once more. I have changed from a young girl who was starting to regain confidence in everyday equestrian tasks to a heartbroken and very teary young girl who only wants to have her handsome little pony back safe and with her!

However, slowly but surely through the comfort of his belongings, photos and a song that brings all of our fabulous memories back, I find every day a little bit easier than the previous one. The here and now is the hardest part of my life so far but I know that no matter what happens I will always have my animals to count on in the moments I need them most, because unlike humans an animal never lies and will never ever resent you or what you are.

On the twenty-fourth of February 2022, early in the morning, I left the field on my pony to go for a hack out on the roads and everything was feeling great until, as I came up past a wall, a van driver drove straight up the back end of me and my pony, Bert. All because he simply wasn't paying attention to what was in front of him on the road.

This happened at the same moment as I did my right shoulder check to see the cars behind me. I felt Bert fully tense through his back and hind end where the van had hit him. Next, I felt the van's wing mirror hit my right thigh. My mind was puzzled and my entire life flashed before my eyes and then...

Bert bolted forward and sideways towards the wall and jumped it. Bert was a superhero in that moment, not only saving his life but mine as well. An absolute rushing wave came through me. We landed in the field on the other side of the wall. Heart beats came like thunderbolts to my chest as the adrenaline kicked in and I realised what had just happened.

The driver of the van did not realize at first that he had even hit us, even though I was screaming at the top of my lungs.

He went to get back in his van after picking up his mirror, but luckily the neighbour stopped him just as my mum arrived. The utter disrespect he showed was disgusting. At first, he said that he thought he had hit a branch, which is ridiculous; I mean, how can you miss a whole entire horse and rider both wearing hi-vis?

I was off trying to calm Bert down to see if he had any injuries. A pounding headache began as I started to realise what the driver had done to my usually calm and bombproof pony. My body finally gave in and the panicky shakes came. Eventually Bert did calm down enough for me to catch him so that the vet could assess him. The vet couldn't find anything too bad at the time, but of course everything was still very fresh for him.

The police did not attend and said that it was a simple case of exchanging insurances, which we were not happy about. My mum moved heaven and earth just to get the police to do something and finally they did. They interviewed the driver and then gave him an option of going straight to court or of taking an intensive driving course. I even had the opportunity to visit The Liverpool Metropolitan Mounted Police through the British Horse Society! But unfortunately, it didn't end there.

During early May 2022 Bert began to act up a little. At first, we thought it was because of his cheekiness and cocky attitude but this behaviour was nothing like he had ever done before. This was pure fear of small things, such as spooking at the sound of a car way off in the distance or at small things on the grass verge like pieces of rubbish, which was way off Bert's usual self.

But on Tuesday the twenty-fourth of May Bert did something horrendous. He barged through the electric fence around the paddock and then straight through the wooden one. He was loose on the road! I tried to lure him into the paddock a first time and failed. He went back onto the road so I shouted his name really loudly and he came cantering back to me and into the paddock, all safe.

However, my mum and I decided that we should send him to a specialist yard to work on rehabilitation and to change his mindset. So we loaded up the horse box all ready to take him on Wednesday. He travelled quite badly and wouldn't settle. We arrived at the yard gates and as we were waiting for the gates to open, we heard an almighty thud from the back of the van but did not think anything of it until we opened the van up and saw that Bert was hanging over the bar into the back.

We got the vet out immediately so that we could get him out in the safest possible way. He had done this because of a psychological trigger caused by the accident. He had split above his eye but luckily there wasn't too much damage and it was a simple case of stitches.

Later that evening we realized that Bert still hadn't gone for a wee, which is not a good sign. We got the vet out to check him over in that area and discovered that the bladder was full to the brim. Thanks to a twenty-four-hour camera we monitored Bert day and night to see if he would wee; however, he did not. The vet was coming out three or four times a day just to empty his bladder for him.

After four whole days Bert did not get any better but only worse. I could see that he was in a lot of pain and decided that the kindest thing for Bert would be to put him to rest.

And I am now left with only memories of Berty. This has been the hardest part of my journey: grief.

I can't say for sure how the future will work out, but what I do know is how I am going to make my future happen. It has only been a month since I lost my Bert and so the wound is still open, but with every day and every minute that goes by it heals just a bit more than the day before. Grief is strange. One day can go by like a flash and everything feels as though it's getting better and then the next feels like it's never ending and all gloomy.

To help with this I usually go straight to his belongings and let my emotions flow, let the words flow out of my mouth and let my tears fall. Or if I am in a situation where I can't do that, such as being in school, I put my earphones in and listen to a song that brings his amazing character and personality close to me and it makes me feel like sometimes he is present with me. I find this is a really good way to help my feelings relax again; I hope that if you try it that it works as well for you as it does for me!

Never ever be ashamed of showing emotion, especially after experiencing the trauma of losing a loved one.

Another coping strategy that works very well for me is doing something that he would have done or something that he enjoyed or something that he would be proud of, and so I began getting a little fitter and going for runs, as what Bert loved to do was run. This is very effective because it allows your mindset to sort of go, *wait, hang on a sec, what am I thinking*? and collect all of the bad things up and put all of that energy into the run. But for you it could be climbing, reading or anything you desire; do it!

Obviously, life is still quite difficult at this point in time. However, each day is a new one for a reason. As a living thing you own a purpose, a reason for existence. Don't ever waste a day because time is a precious gift we are given from above. Animals and people come into our lives for a reason. Some may stay with you forever and some will go but believe me when I say that no matter what, the most special ones of all will stay a part of your life and a part of your future forever and ever, and when the time comes, you will find your special one.

Grief is tough and anyone that says they know how to deal with grief is a liar, because when you grieve over someone it never just goes away like magic, it stays sat at the bottom of your heart like an anchor on the ocean floor for weeks, months and maybe even years. People ask you things like whether you are ok all of the time, and it takes every cell in your body to stop yourself from screaming *shut up and go away* in their faces. I personally hate making a scene and letting people see the opposite side of me – all the crying, anger and pain – but when dealing with grief you never really know what mood you are going to wake up in or how you are going to react to a situation that could possibly bring all of the memories or flashbacks back. I want you to know after reading this chapter that there are other people sitting in the same boat as you right now at this very moment in time.

So now you've heard my story about the accident, losing Bert and how I've been coping with grief. Please try to do what makes you happy, and to spend time with all of those that you love and keep them close, because time is so valuable, now more than ever. So please push through the pain, push through the anger and achieve something amazing out of it. Your entire future depends on you now, and how you deal with it now because all of this that you are going through will shape the future you and what your future will be like. Think as if you are those twenty years older, and have a think about how proud you are going to be making your younger self through fighting all of whatever you are going through now. You'll look back and say *wow, that was really me. I did that; no one else!*

The past is the past now and there is nothing that anyone can do about that. I know it's hard, but it is only the truth. Moving on is the only way forward and take this with a pinch of salt if you will, but your mind will eventually learn to block out all of the sadness and pain because it will build tolerance to what has experienced. My mind is working slowly on this. However, yours may possibly heal quicker, slower or about average. We are all different in our own small ways on this earth and our brains tick differently. One thing we all have in common, though, is a reason; remember that. Look forward to your future, don't dwell on the past and enjoy every moment as much as you can.

be you – not who people want you to be

. . .

Millie

DEAR FRIEND,

If you are struggling with ADHD you might be feeling anxious or even angry. Sometimes you can say things that you don't mean to say – it just comes out – and it might hurt someone's feelings. When this happens, I feel terrible about myself, even though I didn't mean to say it. But when I tell them, "I'm sorry," some can forgive and some can't.

With ADHD you might find yourself fidgeting a lot. When you have ADHD you can't sit still and you always get distracted. When I fidget, I feel like it's because of anxiety, as I never like talking in class and I get this sick feeling in my stomach.

With ADHD you can also experience low self-esteem, so you feel not worthy or capable of achieving things in life. I always say, "I can't do this," or, "I will never be able to do that," and that can make me upset. Feeling unworthy can make you lose yourself, then you might feel depressed. Some days I feel depressed yet other days I can feel creative. You can get mixed emotions like mood swings. Mood swings can be very annoying at points. When I'm happy and having a good time, my mood can change suddenly to me feeling upset or even worried. It can happen at random times and it's not very fun to have. With my ADHD I could be happy but then I feel the need to just get angry at something or I feel like something is not right.

I understand what you are going through right now. You are never going to be alone; there are lots of people, including me, that know what you're dealing with. I used to believe that I would never do well in school, as I got distracted a lot and talked all the time. Also, I used to say to myself that I would never have friends because I talked too much and interrupted people all the time. Then I always asked myself why I was like this. I just wanted to be like everyone else.

However, now that I'm older I don't care what people say or do. I like myself for who I am. I love being different because no one is perfect, only in our own ways. So we are all unique in our own little way.

People think being perfect is having clear skin, having a nice body, being really smart, being popular and even being rich. However, I think that being perfect is just being who you are. It is not about being who people want you to be.

Also, being on medication helped me a lot, so now I don't talk or get distracted as much and I'm doing well in school. I've also got the most amazing friends I could ask for, and I'm happy that they understand that I have ADHD as I told them just so they are aware. I am freer and I can be myself around them.

For me it began in Year Three... that is six years ago. My teacher noticed that I talked a lot and I got distracted a lot. My teacher then talked to my mum about it, but my mum didn't think anything was wrong with me. However, because my teacher had said that she thought I had ADHD my mum booked me an appointment to see someone.

Then three years later, my mum told me about the appointment and that my teacher thought I might have ADHD. I was worried, as I had no idea what ADHD was and I thought I was fine. The next day my mum and I went to see someone.

My mum went into another room to talk to someone about me and I was in a room with a lady who asked me questions about how I feel, about school and normal life. After that, the lady and I played games.

Then my mum came back in and the two ladies went to talk about everything we had discussed, and came back with the results that I had ADHD. I started crying and so did my mum, as she had thought that I was ok.

Knowing that I have it made me think a lot. I wondered if it would ever go away. However, I realise now that it is a part of me now and will forever be. Also, knowing that I have it actually made my behaviour worse. Some said it was because now I can "play on it". However, that's not the case. I don't really know why it got worse. Sometimes I cried at night because of things I had said that I thought might have hurt people. So now I'm a bit more careful with the words I use, but it's not always that easy.

Things started to get challenging in school. As I would get shouted at for talking to my friends a lot. I would also get distracted a lot, so wouldn't really know what we were doing. School has always been challenging for me, even in primary. Spelling is also something I struggle with a lot.

My friendship group is the best, but sometimes we can get into arguments. A lot of the time I say things to them that I don't mean to and it hurts their feelings. Then sometimes they get in a mood with me, and then I start to get in a mood with myself. I start to cry if the things I have said are over text, or if it's in school I just go to the bathroom and cry. Then later on they forgive me, but then I start to over-think and I feel like they don't want to actually be my friend any more.

I also overthink a lot about what my friends really think about me. For example, when I'm being too hyper I get a feeling like they are getting annoyed with me. My sister and I both have ADHD so we argue a lot when we haven't had our medication. I shout at my parents a lot and I hate it, because I always feel so bad after. When I get too hyper around my parents they start to get annoyed and sometimes shout at me. Then I get upset because I can't help it and I'm getting shouted at for something I can't control.

This is the worst part of having ADHD for me. My parents know it's my ADHD but they still shout at me. This is not all the time, which is nice, but sometimes. I can't help getting too excited or hyper and I wish that I could help it, as sometimes I will get too hyper. Sometimes they just tell me to "calm down" just to warn me that I'm starting to get jumpy and excited. My friends don't mind me getting like that, as they know I can't help it and because it makes them laugh. Sometimes I shout at my friends, and I hate that too, because I don't know if I have made them upset. Shouting at people when I do not mean to is the worst part of ADHD, in my opinion.

The people who have made a difference to me are my two best friends, Ella and Deimante. It is really easy to talk to them as we are so close. When I was at my worst moments, Deimante and Ella helped me a lot. I told them everything that I felt and how I was feeling, and they listened to me and gave me advice.

Talking to my friends about how I'm struggling with my ADHD makes me feel less stressed and I know I can trust them both. If I do something they understand that it's my ADHD, and when I talk to them they make me see that it's ok to be different and that I can be myself around them.

Also, my medication helps me a lot as well. When I take it, it makes me less hyper and I can concentrate more. If I didn't have my medication I wouldn't be doing well in school, as I wouldn't be focusing properly. Secondly, I wouldn't be able to go out with my friends because my parents wouldn't trust me to be sensible. So I am so lucky to have my medication.

I have to take them every day if I'm going out. They help me a lot. They make me feel normal, not different. My school helps me as well. When I have tests, I need more time, because I can't process a question that easily. I need some time to think about it before I answer it, so my school gives me more time than others in exams. And that helps me a lot because I don't feel rushed and I can focus more on the test than on the time. Also, when I'm doing my work and my teachers think I look stuck, they come over and ask me, "Is everything ok? You look stuck; let me help you," and that makes me feel like I'm not alone – I have people that can help me.

It has not always been easy, but now my life is easier than ever. My life now is not perfect but not bad. I have amazing friends that I can be myself around. My school has helped me a lot and I really appreciate that. I am doing very well in school, and I'm proud of myself. There are some problems as no one is perfect, but I always find a way to be happy.

If you are going through what I've been through, I just want to tell you that you are never alone; there will always be someone to help you and someone that is going through the same thing. Also, never give up. If you have lost all your friends or you feel like people hate you, there *will* be someone who understands you and appreciates you for who you are.

And always be you. Don't change for anyone. You may feel like you want to change because you're losing all your friends, but you haven't done anything wrong. It's them – if they can't respect that you can't help it or that you act like that, then you should find someone that does. You should never change for anyone, just be you. If you are feeling upset or even scared, then talk to someone. It can be anyone, but it really helps to tell it all out and not bottle it up. They may not understand fully, but they could give you some advice or tips that could become useful in life.

Life will never be easy with ADHD but I promise it will get better in the end. Not perfect but it will get better. I used to cry every day because I was losing friends, and shouting at my friends and family, and I hated myself for it, but now I've got the best friends in the world. I still shout at people but not as much, as I have my medication.

Right now, you might be feeling confused or even sad, but I promise it gets better; you just need to believe that too. You will hopefully get the help and support you need and get friends that respect and like you for being who you are. You will be able to be happy with being different, because I know I am, I have something unique about myself and soon you will think that too. When you find who you are, you will be able to show off your creative mind and how you see things living with ADHD.

I've noticed that people with ADHD see things differently from how normal people do, and I think that's cool. Hopefully your school will help you and support you like my school does. It won't come easy at first, but later on it will start to come easy for you.

perfectly imperfect

. . .

Olivia

DEAR FRIEND,

I'm the youngest in the *Look at Me Now* group. Although I am only eleven, I still have a few stories to tell.

Have you ever felt as if you needed to cover something with makeup? Have you ever felt the need to hide a part of your body because you felt embarrassed by it? Have you felt the need to wear certain clothes to cover up your body in some way because you found parts of you that you disliked?

When you are feeling these emotions, it can be very difficult to deal with. One of the biggest insecurities people have can be the way that they look. When the emotions feel strong you can look around at your friends and they can all look happy with no cares in the world. That can stop you from wanting to share with them how you feel. These feelings can feel very overwhelming. You might not know 'what' you are feeling and so find it hard to talk about. If you don't understand how you feel, it can be even more difficult to know who is best to talk to.

When your body changes in some way, the emotions that you can experience can be like a roller coaster ride. One minute you can feel really sad. I think sadness can be there because your body has changed and does not look the way that it used to.

In the next minute anger can kick in. You feel angry because you did not ask for these changes, and it can feel unfair to look different in some way or have a scar that you didn't ask for.

Frustration may show for you if you think about the scars that are now on your body. You might ask, "Why could my body not just work perfectly?"

We then have social media to add to that mixture of emotions. Social media can allow us to speak with people all around the world, and it can also be very negative because the pictures you see online can be filtered and so you scroll through seeing 'perfect bodies with perfect skin' and this can be a horrid reminder that there are parts of your body that you are not happy with.

You are not alone here. The reason I have written about the emotions of sadness, anger and frustration is because I have felt every single one of them. At times I would avoid looking in the mirror because that showed me parts of me that I didn't like.

I would feel very guilty because people would call me pretty and give me compliments and yet I found it difficult to accept them because I did not feel that it was true.

I felt very angry that I had to go through hurt and pain to have a serious operation. I felt guilty for feeling anger because when I was in the hospital, I saw people who needed more serious treatment than me and that was tough to see as well.

I felt sad because I knew that my body would look different to most other people's that are my age and I did not like the idea that I could potentially stand out.

All of those feelings were very real and raw, and I want to share that I now believe the scars and unique bits of me are a part of my story. They are milestones, and also proof that I have been through difficult things, and I am stronger because of the lessons that they have taught me.

This is my story and how I overcame any insecurities I had. Please know that if I can learn to feel stronger then you can too.

My first insecurity was a birthmark. I have a birthmark down my leg which is big and can sometimes look like a huge purple bruise. I have always been asked what I have on my leg or how I have hurt myself. My friends knew it was there, but it was really horrible meeting anybody new as they would automatically zone in on it.

My second body worry was my scar. There is history of genetic heart conditions in my family. My dad was poorly for a short while and then had open heart surgery when I was three months old.

Then in 2017 my brother had been poorly and needed numerous visits to the doctors. After some in-depth checks we found out that he would also need open heart surgery. He was three years old.

That was two out of four in my immediate family! I had never shown any symptoms like my dad and Joshua but the doctors asked if they could scan my heart to rule out any abnormalities.

I received the invite and went with my parents to the hospital. I lay on the hospital bed feeling really nervous. I had never experienced anything like this before and didn't know what to expect.

The doctor put a freezing cold gel over my chest and began to scan around my heart. It felt like hours, but it was just a few minutes later that he looked at my mum and dad and advised them that I had an identical heart to dad and Joshua… one that needed fixing.

The doctor was very kind and sensitive with me as I did start to panic. On that day when I found out that I needed open heart surgery, there were lots of worries that started going through my mind. I had seen my brother in the hospital bed looking poorly. It was terrifying for me to think about the fact that I was going to be going through that in a couple of months. The fear of being in pain frightened me.

Would I be okay?

What would hospital be like?

How long would I be there?

I missed my friends so how long would I be off school?

During the run up to my operation my teachers would secretly ask me how I was feeling. I always told them I was 'okay' with a smile.

I remember trying to stay brave and telling myself I felt absolutely fine about it. I think I looked and acted fine… all until walking into the anaesthetic room.

I am very lucky that my operation was a success. I was in intensive care for a day and then back on the ward to begin my recovery. I loved eating ice-cream for a few days and the nurses were really funny and very kind to me. I found some days difficult, and some days I felt good but overall my healing was smooth and I was back home in less than a week.

I physically healed very well and quickly. It was the mental struggle that I faced. My body now looked different from before. I was very insecure and hated the way it looked. My scar was red and lumpy and to me it did not look very nice. It comes quite high on my chest so it's something I have to look at all of the time.

The next few months were really difficult for me.

I stopped wanting to go swimming because the top of my swimming costume showed my scar. I went swimming a few times a week with my family and with school and so I felt that I was always making excuses not to go. I hated not having fun as easily as I used to.

I wouldn't wear any tops that had a low neckline. I used to be happy and carefree with my clothes and suddenly I found that to even leave the house I had to put a huge amount of thought into my outfit.

I stopped wanting to wear certain clothes altogether. Jumpers were my favourite as they fully hid my scar and allowed for me to relax a little.

I used to hate people asking me how I felt because I am normally positive and I just didn't like to say that I felt sad in some way. I used to feel so happy and free and now I felt shy, embarrassed and angry. I knew this had to change.

I sat down with Mum and my worries poured out. I spoke about feeling different, I spoke about hating my scar and spoke about how I did not feel happy.

The first and probably most difficult way to feel better was then done. It can feel hard asking for help, but as soon as I had done this I automatically felt as if I had eased it a bit. If there is something that you are worried about, the first thing would definitely be to have one person who you know you can trust. Go to them and share how you feel.

My mum, Joshua and I used to sit and eat breakfast together before school. When I told my mum that I did not feel very confident any more she invented a game. We each had to share three things we love about each other. They could be silly things and serious things so that made it funny. I didn't notice straight away but other people would tell me that I was getting my spark back. I knew I was starting to find the good things about me again and because we played the game every morning, it made me start the day positively.

We would also put our trampette by the door. You cannot jump on a trampoline without laughing and so we always made sure we 'jumped' out of the house each morning feeling happy. (If you don't have a trampoline or a trampette, star jumps will do!)

I started to keep a diary. This helped me feel like I was talking to somebody, and I shared with my diary how I felt that day. I still have the diary now and it is strange looking back through it. It is like a different person has written it. I am very proud of how much I have dealt with and grown.

Put a quote on a mirror that you look in every day. Let that quote be something that makes you smile so that you smile when you look in the mirror and do not feel sad.

I will now only look for my strengths. We all have parts of us that we would possibly change if we were to choose how we look, but think of that as a shadow. We all have a shadow, but we only have to look at it if we want to. Otherwise leave it behind you and focus on what you can love. Find something that you can love. For example: gorgeous hair; strong legs that carry you each day; pretty eyes that can see the good in every day.

Take a deep breath. Know that you are unique and really special, just as you are.

I found a quote that says, "The kindest hearts are the ones with the most scars." This was amazing for me to hear.

Have you heard of the art of Kintsugi? This is a tradition in Japan where if a piece of pottery is broken, the family would put it back together and seal it with gold. This piece of pottery is now worth twice as much because it tells a story. I learnt about this when I was learning about how to look at tough times differently. This is now how I look at my scar. I am me, with a few extra stories to tell.

The thought that made me feel a lot less insecure was the fact that nobody is perfect; everyone has something about themselves that they don't think is perfect. I wear the clothes I like as if the scar was never there now, and I am definitely a lot less conscious of it.

All of the time that that you are worrying is just stealing time away from you that could be spent being happy. Do not waste time hating yourself. Life is very short and you can have so much fun if you let yourself relax and enjoy.

Don't miss time worrying what other people think. Don't miss time feeling insecure because you look different. Imagine how boring it would be looking the same. Don't miss time being unhappy trying to change your body. Enjoy something in every day and love the body you have been given.

being around people you're happy with

. . .

Olivia

DEAR FRIEND,

Going into secondary school is a huge thing for everyone. The jump from primary school where you know everyone to secondary school where everything is new is a big change. This doesn't mean you should be scared about it. Everyone is nervous about this experience. Everyone is experiencing the same thing, but every point of view is different. There will be lots of new people who you won't recognise but in reality, this is a really positive thing. It is important to meet new people even if you never talk to them. These people impact your life more than you think!

The biggest thing people worry about when they go into secondary school is always friends. You're going into a completely new environment and going from being the oldest to the youngest in the school when you have never met half the people within your year group. Therefore, it is understandable that you might be worried about who you will spend your time with. You may be the only person from your primary school going to your secondary school or you may be one of thirty, but the worry about friends is definite in both. It is extremely important to remember that most people will feel the same and even if the friendships don't work, always be kind to everyone because you wouldn't want to be treated any other way by someone in school.

As you go further through secondary school, friendships change a lot. There *will* be quite a few changes even if you think you're friends with the right people and that it won't change. Some people might leave or join your friend group for a variety of reasons, but this is always good if everyone is happy. Talking to new people is a key part in building relationships and it is actually really fun to get to know people who you thought you would never talk to.

I have struggled with friendships because I felt as if I wasn't with people who were making me feel particularly happy. When I felt like this, I didn't know what to do at first, because lots of friendships within my year group were changing and it was all quite confusing. I would be with people that I had never spoken to before, but I enjoyed finding out about people that I knew nothing about.

At the time when I didn't feel particularly happy, it was a bad feeling because I felt as if no one enjoyed being with me or they weren't too interested in me. This made me feel negatively about myself and I know that feeling unwelcome is a hurtful feeling. Now, I realise that the people I was with were maybe not purposely causing me to feel like this and maybe not even realising I did feel like this. When this was happening, my thoughts were quite negative about others and myself. I thought they were purposely not making me feel positively which made me think about the fact that maybe I wasn't similar enough to them to be friends with them.

Without realising it myself, I started talking to new people because other people in my friend group were too. I think it caused all of us to have more interest in each other and we were more open. When this happened, I felt more included and became closer to people in my group, which made me feel happier. I now know lots more about them and every time we see each other we have a good time.

For me, it began around the start of this school year. There was no specific event or time that made anything change but it felt slightly different. The feeling was gradual so it was difficult to notice if anything was actually different at the start and as there was nothing that could've caused it to happen it was confusing in a way. No one was being mean to anyone and we all still talked to each other which is why I thought it was me overthinking the situation.

After a while, I thought about whether other people in my group thought something had changed and felt unincluded because no one was very open at this point. I believed it was due to the new school year starting and school changing in general. I felt quite strange during this time because I didn't know if I or someone else had done something wrong and I didn't feel comfortable asking. My thoughts had changed and I began thinking I had done something because no one else had said anything about feeling like something had changed. This time period felt odd because it didn't last very long. This time caused me to think other people felt everything was normal and nothing had changed.

Things became more challenging because I got to a point where I didn't think anything was going to change and I didn't feel like anyone in my group was there for me to talk to. This led me to the time when I felt the worst because I felt like I should try and spend time with new people although I didn't want to. I didn't want to do this because I couldn't see what had changed from the summer before. Other areas of life got slightly more difficult because I wasn't enjoying any aspect of school and I had no motivation.

Throughout this, I made sure I talked to my family to make sure they knew how I was feeling, and I think this was really helpful to me. As soon as I started to feel like this everyone started to return to how they were before and we all became included again. I think this made everyone instantly feel relief even if they weren't unhappy before because we were all more open and it made school more enjoyable. This was influenced by talking to other people and expanding our social circle. It is so important to include others because it strengthens your relationships.

School has not always been easy but now I spend my time with people who make me laugh every day without fail and don't make me feel negatively. I feel that I have learnt how to deal with the feelings I had before and if I ever had them again, I would know how to deal with them. My advice to someone who feels how I did is to not be afraid to talk to new people. I took the risk and I'm not necessarily good friends with them, but they taught me something and played a key role in my life. If you're in a situation where you feel you can't stop a friendship where you don't feel happy then the chances are over time you will naturally become better friends with people who make you feel happy. This would happen because if you don't feel happy then neither of you are connecting in a way that a friendship connects so never be scared to involve yourself with others.

Everyone has a different experience with making friends. You might find the people you spend the rest of your school life with in the first week or you might not find them for a while. Everyone wants to go to school and spend 90% of their time with people they enjoy being around. These people might be the opposite of you, and you might think you would never be friends with them but there is a strong chance they might be the best friend you've ever had.

Being at high school age children can be quite odd because you're starting to become independent and take risks but it is still quite difficult or confusing sometimes so it is very important to know you can still ask for help. These times can cause you to want to change and that is always okay as long as you're doing it because you want to and not because someone else said you should. If you're changing because of someone else, in the moment you might be convinced it's you who wants to change but in time you may realise it isn't you.

This is never a time to think it can't be changed. If your friends don't make you feel happy then talking to new people that do make you happy is extremely important. Being around these people that you're happy with impacts your mindset in an amazing way. If you start to involve yourself with these people, then you will probably notice that you feel better about schoolwork and general life.

These things are important to being a teenager and building life experiences. The key to having amazing memories is to be yourself from the beginning.

Over the years in secondary school you will experience a lot, but in the end these will be moments you remember forever. Going to school is not something most people love but the experiences are always worth it. Every school offers different opportunities and you may find your life passion if you take the risk and do it. These opportunities build relationships and as you go through school you make friends with more and more people and look forward to some lessons because of the people in them.

If you're looking forward to certain times, make sure you keep in your mind that this is something you enjoy because it could be something you become aware you like and could even help you in a tough time.

Starting a new school can be a worrying time but there is no need to make yourself feel worse about it because it is not worth that. A new school is a new chance so never worry about what could happen, look forward to what will happen. Making new friends and meeting new people is an amazing opportunity. It is character building and makes life exciting. Never worry about people because there is always another person to talk to. Meeting new people can be worrying but don't overthink it – they could be the best thing to ever happen to you! Taking a risk and seeing what happens is always worth it because it will teach you something every time.

do not let your mind bully your body!

. . .

Sian

DEAR FRIEND,

Being a teenager is not easy, being faced with many problems that hit and hit and hit you till you fall and batter you till you're broken. While there are many great things about being a teenager you may be feeling left out, overlooked, not good enough, different, judged… but trust me, everyone has been there. You may not think so, but the most confident person you know could be completely covered up with a false confidence. They might have low self-esteem and just be putting on a brave face.

You could be struggling with your body image, confidence and acceptance of yourself. When you're a pre-teen and teenager you have to accept a lot of change, physically and mentally, and that is not always easy. Physical development hits us all at different ages and at different rates. You may develop a lot sooner than others, gaining curves and boobs (which don't always like to grow to the same size!) or you may feel that others are developing and you still resemble a little girl. What you have to remember is that you may not look like your friend or that popular kid at school or that model on social media, but you look like you and there's only one you.

I have really struggled with my body image in the past and still continue to, but I am improving just like you will. At the age of eleven I wanted to get weight loss surgery for my eighteenth birthday so the boys would like me and so I could look like my friends and wear the clothes they wore, like I had always dreamed. I used to look in the mirror and think to myself, "How could someone be so ugly?" or, "Why would they be friends with me when I look like this and they look like that?" or, "I'm going to be alone forever; no one will love me," and I'd cry.

From the age of eight I wished I looked like other girls and at the age of nine I hated the way I looked. As I became more aware of the world around me I resented the way I looked, but in recent months I've realised that the way I look has never held me back. Instead, I've held *myself* back because of the way I look. So I've decided to push myself out of my comfort zone as much as physically possible on a day to day basis. I used to wear leggings and a jumper every day without fail, no matter the weather, come rain or shine, but now I push myself to have my arms out and if you're very lucky on a hot day you may catch me with my legs out!

When I was very young, I was carefree, confident and quite frankly didn't care what people thought, like most children. As I grew older, I realised that I didn't look quite the same as the other girls in my class. You see, I'm not built like a dancer or a gymnast, I'm built more like a rugby player. I also started developing a lot sooner than most of the girls in my class and I was always one of the tallest. It was highlighted to me that I looked different.

When I saw pictures that were taken on family days out, at parties or at school, I would always ask for them to be deleted or not published on social media because it would be the wrong angle, my clothes didn't fit me right or my cheeks were too big if I was smiling. This caused me a lot of anxiety, although I didn't know that's what it was and with that, I started unknowingly pulling my hair out in hidden sections that caused me to have bald patches. This was discovered one day when my mum was braiding my hair, and when my classmates began commenting on the constant pulling out of my hair which I didn't even realise I was doing. This started as a coping reflex when I was stressed or anxious but soon became a habit that was so hard to break that I can still relapse into it now and need to be made aware that I am doing it.

Things became increasingly difficult when I joined high school with the majority of my primary school peers and I realised that I had no friends due to the dynamics of our friendships changing and finding there was no place for me. In the second month of school, I lost a family member due to tragic circumstances that I witnessed, causing me to become extremely ill mentally and physically. My body totally shut down with shock. I was totally drained and didn't understand why I was feeling like this and so became shut off and distant from my family. The fact that I didn't have any friends to confide in meant I felt totally alone. I was in a very dark place and I wasn't myself, and I took it out on my family and myself. As far as I was concerned nothing anybody did was right or good enough.

Due to that I missed three months of school after only being there for just over a month. Still feeling disconnected from my primary school friends, this wasn't helped when we went into lockdown, which was a daunting and isolating period for everyone. In the midst of this I relied on food for comfort, then afterwards I would feel guilty and wouldn't eat, causing an unhealthy relationship with food that I can still struggle with now. It would always be a handful of biscuits, crisps or a couple chocolate bars that I would grab when no one was looking. If I'd had a bad day, or was tired or bored, it would comfort me and put my nerves at ease and as I'm a creature of habit it caused me to become dependent on the comfort food I would sneak out of the cupboard.

I would get upset and eat but external exercise was restricted and motivation to exercise at home was non-existent during lockdown so like a lot of others I put on some weight. At first, I was in denial when my mum would ask, "Where have the biscuits gone?" I would lie and blame my brother. I knew she knew it was me, but I continued as the comfort at the time was worth it.

When school opened up again people commented that I had put weight on, referring to me as 'the fat one' or 'the big one' making me upset, starting the vicious cycle all over again. My mum always said to never let them see that they had affected me and to hold my head high until I was in a quiet place where I would cry and then try and compose myself to face the rest of the day. The comments hurt because after hearing them a certain number of times you start to believe them. I had never felt so embarrassed to be myself.

At my worst I was so down that I thought it was necessary to try and self-harm. Pulling my hair out didn't seem enough and I considered cutting myself. (I blame social media for this as they say it is a release.) Knowing how bad things had become, my self-loathing hit an all-time low and I started pulling my hair out again but luckily my mum noticed and helped me to get through it. Do you have someone close that could be there for you?

I haven't reached the end of my journey; in fact, I am right in the middle of it. One thing I have learned is that everybody needs a moment of realisation (a lightbulb moment!). This is a moment when they understand that bottling up all their emotions and feelings doesn't help but actually makes things a lot worse. My lightbulb moment was when my English teacher told my class that her weight had never held her back, dictated or stopped her from doing or achieving anything in her life, so why should we?

Following that, I rediscovered my passion for horses. I started working at two different yards: one of them is on the weekends, alongside other teenagers that have the same interests and so my friendship group has now increased. At the other yard I have been given responsibility for six horses one evening a week to help the owner out, but this also shows me that I am trustworthy and capable. Animals are a great help for me. They listen (most of the time) and they don't judge or care what you look like. I have found that my dogs and the horses are a way to escape reality and I can just be me. They are a newfound comfort; they love me for who I am and give me a reason to be active.

Another thing I tried was Thai Boxing. My brother had started before lockdown and thoroughly enjoyed it but I was too insecure to go... so I thought I'd challenge myself and give it a go. The idea of it was a lot easier than actually turning up and walking through the gym door.

I went with a friend who just strolled in and got stuck in but when I saw a gym mainly full of big men and boys my own age, I automatically felt very vulnerable and insecure.

My mum didn't force me to join the class but did make me stay at the gym as it wasn't fair on my friend to be left there on her own. While I sat there and watched, members of the class encouraged me to join in and were so welcoming and friendly that I couldn't say no, and I haven't looked back since! It has proved to me that I shouldn't be so quick to judge people and that I hope people will be less quick to judge me!

I have learnt many things on my journey so far, one of them being that not everything has to be perfect. Putting too much pressure on myself and creating unnecessary stress was such a drain physically and mentally and I have now learnt to give myself a break. We can't control everything or everyone, as much as we'd like to, but we can control ourselves and how we react and deal with situations.

For example, we can't control other people's opinions but we can control how we respond to them. I have to remind myself that when people try to put me down, they are actually just as insecure as I am and they're trying to make themselves feel better by making me feel small. It is hard but I have to remember to not react and to actually feel sorry for them. I can then walk away with my head held high knowing I've been the bigger person.

Our self-worth is ten times more valuable than anyone else's opinion of us which is why it is so hard when we are feeling down and vulnerable, as we can also be the most critical person towards ourselves. So if it is possible, surround yourself with positive people, whether that is in school or not. Be true to yourself and people will like you for you, rather than trying to mould yourself to fit in with others that don't care. I have learnt to be myself and my approach is that if people don't like me then they shouldn't waste my time.

I may seem like I have a chip on my shoulder, but I am not mean or nasty. I just stand up for myself and for others who haven't found their voice yet, as I have been in their position. I now try to look on the brighter side of life and am able to laugh at myself if things don't go the way I planned as I am human and make mistakes. High school is a very small steppingstone in life but at a very vulnerable time when everyone is trying to find themselves and where they fit in. It's not an easy or a quick fix, but if you put the time and effort into trying to accept yourself, then anything is possible.

The hardest questions to be able to answer are…

- What are your strengths?
- Tell me three things you like about yourself…
- Are you too hard on yourself?
- What/who are you grateful for?

If you can't answer these questions, then you need to start being kinder to yourself. Maybe look at yourself from another person's point of view and see what your closest people love about you and then start to love yourself. It's a cliché,

I know, but it's true! At this moment you could be reading this and feeling like a lost cause, that there's no point trying. But if you can learn anything from reading this book it's that you're not alone and there is hope for you.

so many feelings go unsaid

. . .

Yazmin

DEAR FRIEND,

My name is Yazmin and I want to write about how my behaviour over the last few years in school started to effect both my school and home life in a really negative way.

I definitely haven't found school easy over the last few years, probably starting at the end of primary school and carrying on through my transition into high school, and this caused me to feel really angry inside. You might also be feeling angry and frustrated inside and I totally understand that the pressure of school life and friendship groups aren't easy to handle and so I want to help you to manage your anger better than I did.

I bottled my emotions up inside and didn't tell anyone how I felt, and I want you to know that regardless of what is causing your anger and frustration, speaking out with somebody you trust can really stop those negative emotions taking control.

I have learnt a lot over the last few years about my emotions and how best to deal with them and I hope that my story can help you to do the same. You may want to lash out or behave badly like I did but I've learnt now that it's important to manage those emotions instead. This is an important part of my story as I felt the need to self-harm in order to try to deal with the emotions that were bottled up inside, but I've learnt that this only makes things worse. I went down this path for a while and I'm still working on these emotions, but I want you to know there are different ways to help with any anger you might be feeling caused by any pressure in life

I firstly want you to know that you are not alone if you are feeling any negative emotions inside. You may be feeling anger, frustration, and sadness just like I did. But trust me when I say that these emotions are ok when you deal with them properly, as I have now learnt to. I thought I was the only person on the planet feeling the way I did.

The worst part about this time in my life was keeping how bad I felt to myself. This allowed those negative feelings to take over and become much worse than they actually were.

I was very aware that these emotions were bottled up inside and I regularly used to worry that I would never get rid of them and feel any better. This used to make me feel frustrated and angry inside and so I then used to act horribly to my family and friends, either with unkind words or I would just choose to be distant and ignore them.

When I started high school, I really thought things would be ok, and that I would behave well – I never in a million years thought I'd start acting naughtily. I was good between starting in September until around December time but then one of my close friends didn't want to stay friends with me – she had found other friends and wouldn't even acknowledge me. This really hurt me inside. I understand that friendships drift apart, but I just wasn't expecting it at all so my way of dealing with my hurt inside was by starting to be mean to her by calling her names, pushing her and just being really unkind. Rather than feeling sad any more, it felt fun to me as the person who had made me upset was now the person getting upset. I did eventually get caught behaving so badly but getting told off didn't change things. At first getting told off would upset me and make me cry, but then I decided that it was worth it as I felt better by being the one in control and so I stopped caring.

About a month later I then started to skip lessons and I also started getting gobby with teachers. One day I was being naughty and I even swore at my teacher and that got me excluded.

I wasn't proud but again, I didn't mind it. I think in some ways I liked being the naughty one because I liked the attention it got me in school – I felt popular.

All of this bad behaviour started having an impact at home and my home life then started to change – I was always getting shouted at for things that I wouldn't even think were that bad. I did try to behave but because I felt like I was getting in trouble for the littlest of things and seemed to be getting nowhere, I ended up deciding to stop trying and to go back to this route of being naughty. I can't lie to you all, although I thought this was the way things had to be, always getting shouted at actually made me feel really sad and stressed inside.

Through all of this mess I'd now got to the point where I felt there was no way out. I felt miserable in school and at home, and I couldn't seem to stop the bad behaviour. This is where things took a really bad turn and I decided to start cutting myself. I only started with doing a little bit with plastic and it was hardly deep. I did stop for a while but then I'd do it again, on my arm again, but not too deep. I found a sort of comfort from doing it, so I started doing it until it bled. Then I moved on to doing it on my thigh. Today, my left arm is covered in scars which I'm not proud of but at the time it was all I felt like I could do. I felt a sense of relief from everything.

Eventually I got caught got caught by teachers in my school and they really wanted to understand why. I never knew what to say because I worried that once I started talking, I wouldn't be able to stop.

I also started getting angry. I started being mean to my closest friends and losing them.

I didn't want to talk about it in school or at home because at the time I felt like it was because of the situation with them that I felt like this. Now I know that keeping the anger inside was the problem and not everyone around me.

This was one of the most stressful times of my life and I felt like I had no one to turn to or talk to.

So what's changed for me? I realised inside that I was going down the wrong path. Rather than any of these behaviours or self-harming helping me, they were only making me more upset and nothing was changing.

The school finding out meant that my mum found out and although I find it difficult to talk about it with my mum, the fact she knows now has helped everything be out in the open.

At the time I felt like I had no control, and I was just scrambling with all these emotions. Now a couple months later I'm doing better. I'm doing better in school and I feel a bit better mentally. I'm definitely not one hundred percent, but I understand my emotions a lot better and I know I'll be ok. Being part of the Soul Sisters group has helped me a lot. It's given me confidence to speak to people which is much better than keeping things to myself.

My advice to anyone having a tough time, whether that be at school or in their home life, would be:

- Always talk to a friend that you trust. School friendships are tricky anyway, and speaking to somebody you do not trust could make it worse.
- Please know that there is always somebody there for you that wants the best for you – whether that is a teacher or a member of your family.
- Keeping your feelings bottled up doesn't help. At one point there will be too much to keep in and it has to come out in some way.
- Self-harming doesn't help. It may feel good at the time but you will get scarred and it doesn't actually solve the problem you faced anyway.
- You may never love school, but you have no choice but to be there so my advice is to just get your head down and deal with it.

Sometimes I can still feel angry inside, but I really try my best to not be angry with my words. Sometimes in school I know I need to ask if I can step outside or take a minute. I then try and remind myself that if I get angry it's going to get me in more trouble and not help anything.

I have been self-harm free for nearly two months now and even though I have had lots of ups and downs, I'm still trying my best. Now I speak to my best friend if I'm having a hard day, rather than keeping those emotions inside.

People ask me how I am and now I'm trying to be honest with how I feel. No one ever asked me that before and the truth is I'm not always feeling great but talking really helps. My friends have helped me tons by just being there. They somehow always seem to put a smile on my face no matter how bad my day is. I still think school is really tough, I find it mentally draining and it can feel quite depressing, bringing up all these negative amotions and anger. However, I know I can deal with these feeling now and I remind myself that I get to see my friends for six hours and this really helps me through it.

But through all this I have realised the importance of having someone to talk to – without this I don't know where I'd be right now. If you are feeling like I am, please find someone you trust to talk to. It could be your family, your friends or even a teacher. It really does help a lot. I know it's not easy but trust me you'll get through it.

My life is getting better slowly every day. Obviously, we all have our ups and downs, but you need to know that's ok. Through my friends supporting me, I'm now doing the same for them, looking out for them when they are going through problems, and this has really helped.

Whatever you are going through in life, please remember to reach out and don't keep those emotions bottled up inside. Everything always gets better; it just takes time.

Printed in Great Britain
by Amazon

17035102R00054